McCrory's Developmental Milestones Express Tool Kit

By

Tammy McCrory LLP, BCBA

Published & Distributed By:

McCrory Toolkits
MICHIGAN

2022

DISCLAIMER: MUST READ

MESSAGE FROM TAMMY MCCRORY

Dear Parents and Guardians,

I really want to help your child learn and grow in the best way. I know parents are very important for this. So, I'm excited to tell you about ways you can help your child grow.

This guide and the suggested items are primarily designed for children learning at the age of 1 to 3 years. Sometimes, a child's learning age isn't the same as their real age, and that's okay. Keep this in mind when reviewing the information.

The guide and suggested tools provide fun activities to do with your child each day. These activities are meant to be fun and helpful for your child's growth.

Please remember, this isn't the same as therapy or medical help. You should still pursue or continue any treatments that your child needs. This guide and suggested tools are here to provide you with ideas and tips to support your child's learning at home and ensure their safety.

My main goal is to make being a parent easier and to help you learn more about you child's development.

I hope this kit makes it easier for you to teach your child new things with lots of love, patience, and positivity.

Happy Parenting!

Tammy McCrory MA LLPBCBA LBA

TABLE OF CONTENTS

McCrory's Developmental Milestones Express Tool Kit

PROMPTS FOR PARENTS TO AID THEIR CHILD'S GROWTH

As parents of a child who are 1-3 years old, you are in a very important time for your child's growth. They are growing quickly, learning how to show their feelings, and starting to think in new ways. To help your child during this special time, it's great to play with them in ways that make them curious and want to learn.

Parent's Interaction Prompts

Small Balls

You can play with your child by rolling or throwing a plastic ball. It's a fun way to help them move around more and pay attention to the game. This game is good for kids 1 year and older.

Flute

By playing with a flute, your toddler can make their own music. This can help them get better at moving their fingers, listening & paying attention to sounds. Toddlers who are at least 1 year old can enjoy this.

Push Car

This toy is a fun way to teach your toddler by naming parts on the car. It also helps them move around and play. This toy is good for kids starting at 12 months old.

Maracas

Maracas are another music tool your toddler can shake and make noise with. They're good for toddlers 1 year old and above.

Parent's Interaction Prompts

Flashlight

Using a toddler-safe flashlight as a teaching tool can engage and develop skills such as attention, curiosity, motor skills, and early scientific concepts in toddlers starting from around 18 months old. Please make sure you do not give the child the tool to play with but use it as a teaching tool, and the child should always be supervised.

Mirror

Looking at themselves in a mirror can help your toddler understand who they are. They can also copy faces or movements they see in the mirror. This gadget is good for toddlers of all ages.

Rubber Ducky

Rubber duckies can make bath time more fun. Your toddler can play with them in water and learn about daily habits. This toy is good for toddlers of all ages.

Bubbles

Your toddler can practice recognizing shapes and move around more while trying to catch bubbles. This activity is good for 1-year-olds and older.

Parent's Interaction Prompts

Stack & Count Cups or Blocks

Your toddler can practice motor movements, learn about different sizes, and improve their hand-eye coordination by stacking these cups or blocks. This activity is suitable for toddlers aged 1 year and older.

Toddler Toothbrush

Using their own toothbrush can teach your toddler about cleanliness and taking care of themselves. This tool is good for toddlers 1 year old and above.

Puzzles

Puzzles are a good way to teach problem-solving. Your toddler can also improve their hand movements and learn to recognize different things. This activity is good for 2-3 year olds.

UNDERSTANDING KEY GROWTH MILESTONES

Keeping track of your child's growth stages, or developmental milestones, is really important. It helps you see if there might be something wrong. Then, you can talk to a doctor or a health professional about it. If your child needs help, getting it early can make a big difference. It helps them now and later in life to be their best. Remember, every child grows at their own pace. Some might be faster or slower than others.

EXPECTED MILESTONES FOR 12-18 MONTH OLD CHILDREN.

Every mom and dad want their child to do really well. One way to help is by guiding them to meet special goals for their age. These goals are like guidelines that tell what your child should be able to do at a certain age.

12 months

- Walking all by themselves or with a little help
- Doing simple things like waving hi or shaking their head no
- Seeing everyday things and being able to point at them
- Listening and doing easy directions, like when someone says come here
- Speaking a few easy words like mama and dada
- Loving to play simple games like peekaboo
- Being really close and liking their main caregivers like mom and dad
- Being curious and exploring their surroundings by touching and holding onto things.

18 months

- Walking by themselves and starting to run
- Starting to talk in short sentences
- Can show all feelings
- Likes make-believe games, like feeding a baby doll
- Listens and understands simple things like pick up the toy
- Can point to body parts when asked
- Likes some foods, toys, and people more than others

6

EXPECTED MILESTONES FOR 2-3 YEARS OLD CHILDREN

2 Years-Old

- They can say small sentences with two or three words.
- They start to learn the names of colors and shapes.
- They start to play near other kids but not really with them.
- They might not always listen because they want to do things by themselves.
- They can sort things based on what shape or color they are.
- They can do simple things like pick up a toy and put it on a table.
- They can climb on furniture and get down by themselves.
- They get better at using their hands and fingers to do things like turning knobs or opening lids.

3 Years-Old

- Talks in a way that others can understand easily
- Can put on and take off clothes with a little help
- Starts learning to share and wait for their turn
- Getting better at moving around, can ride a three-wheeler or kick a ball
- Loves to play pretend games
- Starting to feel sorry or happy for others
- Can count till 3 or more and knows what is more and what is less
- Becoming more independent, like brushing teeth or using the toilet by themselves.

If your child is not doing things that most children their age do, it could be a sign they need extra help. You should talk to their doctor about it. The doctor can check on your child and give you advice on what steps to take next.

USING AGE-APPROPRIATE TOYS & GADGETS TO PROMPT YOUR CHILD'S GROWTH

Choosing toys and gadgets that are just right for your little one's age is important because they can help your child learn and grow. For toddlers aged 1 to 3 years old, it's great to pick items that will encourage them to use their imagination, explore the world around them, and improve their physical abilities.

Playing with 1-2-year-olds using fun activities can enhance their focus and talking skills by discussing colors, shapes, animals, and people. Continuing play as they turn three or older helps improve their conversation abilities and maintain their concentration.

Attention

Suggested Tools: Flute, Bubbles, Flashlight

Getting your child's attention is really important when you talk to them. If they are not paying attention, it's difficult for them to learn what you are trying to teach them. Here are some tips to help you get your child's attention

Use the recommended tools to gain your child's attention:

- Flute - You can blow softly on the flute to make fun sounds and get your toddler's attention.

- Bubbles - Blowing bubbles is a lot of fun. Do this often with your child. This is a sure way to get their attention and they'll love it.

- Flashlight- Don't shine a flashlight straight into your child's eyes.
    - Use your hands to create shadow figures on the wall. Shine the flashlight beam on the floor and encourage your toddler to follow it or step on it.

- This will get them interested in looking around more.

When talking with your kid, make sure to look into their eyes. If your kid does not look back into your eyes while talking to talk to their doctor for advice.

Children learn how to make big moves, like grabbing, when they are very young. Around six months old, they can start to grab items. By the time they are nine to twelve months old, they are usually really good at it. But all kids learn at different speeds. Playing games and doing fun things with them can help them learn these moves better and faster.

GROSS MOTOR

Suggested Tools: Maracas, Stacking Cups or Blocks, & Toy Car

There are many fun things your child can do to get better at moving and using their hands.

Teach your child how to enjoy these toys. You can help them learn about cause and effect. If they find it hard, you can demonstrate or even guide their hand. This way, they can have fun and learn at the same time.

- Shaking maracas is a cool activity because children can make awesome sounds. It helps them get better at using their hands and arms. They can shake the maracas fast, slow, up, or down!.

- Playing with blocks or stacking cups is really fun! It's like a game that can also make their hands stronger. Children can build high towers, drop blocks into cups, and create anything they think of!

- When children play with toy cars, their parents can help them learn the right way to play. They can show them how to hold the toy car and how to push or pull it correctly

Always be patient when your child is learning something new. Getting mad can scare them from trying again. If they don't know how to do something, that's fine! Just guide them.

Children as young as six months old can learn a lot just by looking at people and playing with books. When they reach their first birthday, they are often able to copy the faces others make. Using a mirror is a great idea because it lets them see their own faces and discover more about who they are.

SELF-IDENTIFICATION

Suggested Tools: Mirror

Using mirrors and other tools can help your child understand and recognize themselves better.

Mirrors can help kids learn and grow. When they see themselves, they understand they are unique. This can help them think, remember and focus better.

- Show your child the mirror.

- Ask them who they see in the mirror.

- Use this moment to talk and help them learn that they are looking at themselves.

- Make faces that are funny, sad, or surprised and ask your child to make them too.

- Remember, your child might only make faces back or not react with words or at all until they get bigger.

It's alright if your child isn't responding yet. Keep encouraging them, they may enjoy it. Repeating actions can help them learn to talk and understand better.

Little ones begin learning how to talk when they are about 6 months old by babbling and making noises. However, from the time they are 2 until they are 7 years old, they pick up many more words and start to get better at understanding language. Most importantly, give your child chances every day to practice talking and to chat about what's around them.

LANGUAGE DEVELOPMENT

Suggested Tools: Your Voice, Reading, Asking Questions, Identifying Objects

To help you teach child language, think about using these helpful tricks.

- Help your child learn new words by naming things around them, like a four-legged chair or the color of their clothes.

- You can also show them pictures in books or on the TV, and talk about what they see.

- When talking about feelings, use easy words to explain how you feel, and slowly teach them new words.

- Show them how to talk properly by using hand gestures with your words, and repeating words so they become easy for them to remember.

- During reading time, use books with rhymes and repeated sounds to help them learn new words.

Encourage your kid to talk more by asking them questions

A 1-year-old can also use actions to communicate, like shaking their head to say no or pointing at something they want. They might be able to answer simple questions like:

- *Where is your nose/mouth/eyes?*
- *Do you want more food?*
- *Can you give me the ball?*
- *Can you point at the cat/dog?*
- *Do you want a bath?*

12

Kids who are 2 years old can answer simple questions like yes or no. They can say the names of things they know and listen to easy instructions:

- *Do you want juice or milk?*
- *Is this a car?*
- *Can you show me where your shoes is?*
- *Are you hungry?*
- *Where is your teddy bear?*
- *Do you want to go to the park?*
- *What sound does a cat make?*
- *Where is your nose/mouth/eyes?*
- *Do you want more food?*
- *Can you give me the ball?*
- *Can you point at the cat/dog?*

At 3 years old: At this age, kids start to get better at answering tricky questions. They learn new words and can talk more. They can often answer easy questions like Who?, What?, Where? and Why?

- *What did you do at daycare or school today?*
- *Where did you leave your toy car?*
- *Who is your favorite cartoon character?*
- *Why are you sad?*
- *What's your friend's name?*
- *What color is this ball?*
- *Can you count these blocks for me?*
- *Where do we put dirty clothes?*

Ensure daily conversation with your child to improve their communication skills.

Every child grows and learns at their own pace, and their responses to questions are based on what they know. The ages mentioned are just averages. If you're concerned about your child's communication or understanding, speak with their doctor.

From the time they are babies, children begin to learn how to play. They start with simple actions like shaking a toy or touching various things. As they grow up, they play with more challenging toys and begin to play with other children. Between the ages of 1 and 3, they become better at playing and their games become more detailed.

Play

Suggested Tools: Balls, Stacking Items, Toy Car, Rubber Ducks

Playing and having fun every day is good for your kid's body and brain to grow.

Small Balls

- First, show your little one how to hold and let go of the ball.
- Then, slowly teach them how to pass or toss the ball to you, which is good for their movement.
- As they get better, teach them harder things like catching and kicking.
- For learning, talk about and show them the differences in how big, how it feels, and what color different balls are.

Stacking Cups or Blocks

- Show your little kid how to put the cups or blocks on top of each other and how to take them apart.
- Let them try to do it by themselves, this will help them with moving their fingers better and coordinating their hands and eyes.
- Use the cups to show them which one is big and which one is small.
- Help them learn their colors by telling them the color of each cup or blocks.

Remember, the goal is not just to have fun, but also to help your child learn new things, be curious, and behave nicely through playing.

Toy Cars

- Let your kid play with the cars by pushing and pulling them.
- Make pretend stories or paths for the cars.
- Help your child figure out how to get the cars past little roadblocks.
- Explain what happens when cars bump into each other or slide down a ramp.

Rubber Ducks

- Rubber ducks are really fun to play with during bath time. You can teach your child how to play the 'splash' game with them to get better at using their hands and eyes together.
- Teach them how the duckie can float in the water. This will show them how things can float.
- Help your child to think up fun stories with the ducks. This will make bath time even more fun and help them use their imagination.

Let your child play at their own speed and don't make them play if they don't want to - playing should always be fun and something they enjoy doing.

Children can usually begin to play with easy puzzles when they turn 2. This is when they learn to know shapes and colors which are important to play with puzzles. But remember, not all kids might be ready at the same age. Always make sure the puzzles are just right for their age and have no tiny parts that could be dangerous if swallowed.

Puzzle & Stacking

Suggested Tools: wooden shape or peg puzzles

Playing with puzzles, stacking, and sorting games can help strengthen and enhance your child's brain.

- Learn Shapes: Help your little one learn about different shapes and where they go in the puzzle. Start with easy shapes, like circles and squares, before trying the harder ones.

- Show and Tell: Sit with your child and work on the puzzle together. Show them how each piece goes in its place and explain why it fits there.

- Cheer Them On: Always say well done when your child places a piece correctly. It makes them feel happy and encourages them to keep going.

- Take Your Time: Remember to be patient. The main thing is to have fun and learn how to solve problems. There's no need to rush. Your child might need more time, and that's completely okay.

Always remember, every kid learns in their own time. The main thing these activities should do is to make learning fun and playful for your little one.

Children usually start to understand pictures in a book when they are around one and a half to two years old. But remember, every child is different! It also depends on how often they see books or pictures.

RECOGNIZING ITEMS

Suggested Tools: Pictures, books, and everyday items they encounter.

Helping toddlers learn to identify objects from pictures can be a lot of fun! Here are some methods they might enjoy.

- Choose Bright Pictures: Select photos featuring everyday items such as cars, trees, cats, balls, food, toys, and clothes. Ensure these pictures feature bright and simple colors, making it easier for your toddler to see and recognize them.

- Show the Picture to Your Toddler: Present one picture at a time to your toddler, making sure to articulate clearly and slowly what is depicted in the image.

- Discuss the Picture: Engage in a discussion about what is observed in the picture. Point out its color, size, usage, or typical location. This process aids your child in learning about their surrounding environment.

- Use Actual Objects: After showing a picture to your toddler, proceed to show them the actual object that was depicted. For instance, if you presented a picture of a banana, then offer them a real banana to observe next.

Remember that every child learns at their own speed. Be patient, give lots of praise, and keep trying are the keys to helping them learn.

For little kids who are 1 to 3 years old, learning to do things by themselves is important. These are things like getting dressed, eating by themselves, and cleaning up toys. Doing these things helps their brains grow, helps them get good at using their hands and fingers, and makes them feel proud of what they can do.

Daily Living Skills

Suggested Tools: kids toothbrush & child-safe utensils

Here's an easy guide to help you help your kid learn important skills

- Self-feeding: Start by letting your child use their fingers to grab soft, easy-to-hold food.

- Using Spoons and Forks: When they seem ready, show them how to use a spoon and fork. Say good job when they try, even if they make a mess.

- Getting Dressed: Pick clothes that are easy to put on, like pants with stretchy bands or shirts with big buttons.

- Brushing Teeth: At first, you will brush their teeth for them. Slowly, let them try with you watching, giving tips and helping them learn the right way.

- Washing Hands: Teach your child why it's very important to wash their hands, like before eating and after going to the bathroom.

- Bedtime: Help them get ready for bed by doing things like putting on pajamas, brushing teeth, and reading a story to show it's time to sleep.

- Sleeping Well: Make sure their room is good for sleeping and keep the same bedtime and wake-up time every day.

Always remember, when teaching kids new stuff, be very patient. Always say nice things about their tries and keep them happy about their work. Let them practice safely and it's okay if they mess up a bit.

Potty training usually starts between 18 months and 3 years old. However, every child is different and some may be ready earlier or later than this range.

Potty Training

Suggested Tools: potty training chair (you will need to purchase)

Look for Signs. Before starting, see if your child is ready. They might tell you they're wet or want their diaper changed.

You can guide them with the following steps:

- Get the Bathroom Ready: Buy a small potty or a special seat for the big toilet. Have soft toilet paper or wipes just for kids ready too.

- Show Them the Potty: Explain how the potty is used and that it's just for them. Have them sit on it with clothes on to get used to it. Use easy, happy words to talk about the potty.

- Have Potty Times: Take your child to the potty regularly. You can try every two hours. This helps them learn the habit of going.

- Cheer for Good Tries: Give a clap or sticker if they use the potty. This makes them want to try again.

- Be Okay with Accidents: Mess-ups will happen. Don't be upset. Just clean up and remind your child that next time they can try the potty.

- Stay Consistent: Keep following the routine, even when you're out or busy. Consistency helps your child learn faster.

Remember, it's important not to rush a child to use the toilet before they are ready. Each child grows differently and at their own speed. Not all children are ready to learn to use the toilet at the same time.

We can start teaching babies how to be nice and kind. Even if they don't understand yet, showing them good behavior helps them learn as they grow. Children start acting good on their own when they are 2 or 3 years old.

Pro-Social Behaviors

Suggested Tools: role models and imaginative beings

Teaching children to behave nicely is good because it helps them to be kind, work well with others, and understand feelings. This will make them good at making friends and dealing with feelings when they grow up.

- Kindness: Tell your child to treat their teddy bears well, so they'll be kind to others.

- Making Friends: Playing with teddy bears can help kids use their imagination and get better at playing with friends.

- Being Polite: Teach your children to use 'please' and 'thank you'.

- Good Behavior: Show your child how to be friendly, speak nicely, and fix problems without arguing.

- Saying Sorry: Remind kids to apologize if they make a mistake.

Remember, kids learn a lot by seeing what others do. So, it's very important for grown-ups to always be nice so kids can learn well.

PARENTING STYLES MATTERS

For parents of 1-3 year-olds, this period is full of joy and challenges. Your toddler is exploring and learning rapidly. As their guide, show them love, patience, and understanding to shape their development positively. Your interactions now are crucial for their growth into kind and confident individuals. Embrace this time with love, laughter, and shared learning.

Know Your Parenting Style

Authoritative Parenting

This kind of parenting is thought to be the best. These parents make guidelines, but they also care about their children's feelings. They spend a lot of time talking with their children. This can help children grow up to be happy, successful, and brave.

Permissive Parenting

Some parents don't have guidelines and let their children do anything they want. They try to be like their children's buddies. However, this might result in children not learning how to be responsible or realizing that they can't always have what they want.

Uninvolved Parenting

This is about when moms and dads don't play or talk much with their kids. They might not know what's going on in their kids' day or school. This could make kids feel like they're not being noticed and they might feel sad.

Authoritarian Parenting

These moms and dads are strict and make all choices. They have lots of rules and don't always explain why. Kids in this situation might feel shy or scared to make mistakes.

Every parent is different. They might have various methods for raising their children. The most important thing is love. When children feel loved, they feel secure, brave, and sure of themselves.

FREE AND FUN IDEAS TO PROMPT YOUR CHILD'S GROWTH

There are lots of fun things you can do with your little kid in the places around you that don't cost any money at all. These activities are fun and can help your kid learn and grow!

Free and Fun Ways to Engage Your Child

Expose Your Child

To help your child learn fast, let them try new things like meeting new friends, going to new places, hearing new sounds, and feeling different feelings. This can help them know what to do later.

If you don't have much money, you can still have fun for free. You could visit your local park. There might also be fun spots like community centers. Plus, some churches have fun events for families.

Physical Activities

To keep your child healthy, don't let them sit too much in strollers or watch lots of TV, especially if they're under two years old. Instead, let them play with toys on a small table or floor, encourage them to dance and move around. This will help them learn to move and play better.

Read & Talk

You should read with your child five times a week and chat with them daily. When talking, look into their eyes. Pick books they find fun and interesting. You can borrow books from the library or buy cheap ones at used book stores. Some places even give out free books. You can also look online for free books. It's very important to talk and read with your kids.

Teach Words

Help your child learn words for their feelings. This lets them talk about their day and ask for help when they need it. Sometimes, when children don't know how to say how they're feeling, they might act out, like hitting or throwing things. If parents respond kindly to this (like saying that must be tough!), kids can learn better ways to express their feelings.

Free and Fun Ways to Engage Your Child

Label Objects

Knowing how to name things can make kids smarter and it's really fun. When kids give names to things, they understand everything around them, like toys, pets, and people, much better. This helps them to speak well and learn new words. A fun way to learn names can be with stickers or pointing at body parts, foods, and animals.

Give Happy Cheers & Kind Words

We know that saying kind things makes children feel happy and do better. We should tell children they're doing well when they act nicely. We should always say nice things to children and tell them to keep it up. We can even give them a small prize when they do a good job.

Prompt Your Child

A prompt is like a helpful clue you give someone to guide them to do the right thing. It's like when you give hints to your little kid to help them learn and grow. Prompts can help them decide things on their own, learn to talk better, do good things, solve problems, and understand what happens when they do certain things.

Teach Safety

Explain to your toddlers about rules in a simple way. Teach them about the differences between good touch and bad touch, and tell them why it's important to have personal space. Make sure when you teach about safety, you don't scare them, but make them careful. Also, teach them how to be safe when they are outside, like when they are in the park or crossing the road. Remember, it's good to start teaching them these things at an early age.

CHILD SAFETY TIPS

It's very important to protect your child from anything bad or harmful that can hurt them. Do things to keep them safe from sickness and things that might be bad for their health. Make sure they grow up in a safe and healthy place.

Keep Your Child Safe

Physical Environment Safety

To keep your child safe at home, remove anything that can cause harm. This means getting rid of sharp items, things that can easily break, and cleaning supplies. It's also important to make the house safer. You can do this by putting covers on stairs and electrical outlets to prevent falls or electric shocks. This will help prevent accidents.

Firearm Safety

To keep everyone safe, it's very important to always keep guns and other dangerous things locked away where little kids can't reach them. Even a quick mistake could cause a very sad accident.

Exposure to Lead Paint

Lead-based paint is a type of paint often found in old houses. It can be harmful to children if they eat or breathe it in. So, parents need to learn about lead poisoning and how to handle paint chips and dust to keep their kids safe.

Smoke Exposure

Making your home smoke-free is really important because breathing in other people's smoke is bad for kids' health. If we don't smoke inside and make sure to smoke far away from kids when outside, we can help them avoid problems like breathing trouble and lots of ear infections.

Watch out for dangers, like things, people, or situations, that could hurt your child.

Keep Your Child Safe Continued

Protect From Abuse

We have to keep child safe. This means protecting them from anything that can hurt their bodies, feelings, or personal space. We need to learn how to tell if a child is being hurt and what to do if that's happening.

Mold and Pest Control

To stop mold from growing, keep your house clean and dry. Also, getting rid of bugs and pests helps to keep a safe and healthy space for a baby to live in.

Socialization

Keeping a toddler away from people who use drugs or are mean and hurtful can make it less likely for them to get hurt or abused.

Disease Prevention

To keep the child healthy, it's very important to get them their shots on time and take them for health checkups often. It's also really important to learn about common sicknesses kids can get and what signs to look for.

Keep your child safe by knowing about dangers and taking steps to stop them. Feel less worried by learning all you need to make sure your child is safe.

UNDERSTANDING AND ADDRESSING DEVELOPMENTAL DELAYS

Although most children meet their developmental milestones on time and as expected, some children may have a condition that delays their growth. This means you need to seek expert help to assist them in reaching their full potential. If you identify delays and know that your child is behind and you are denied services by an expert, continue seeking services elsewhere for a second opinion.

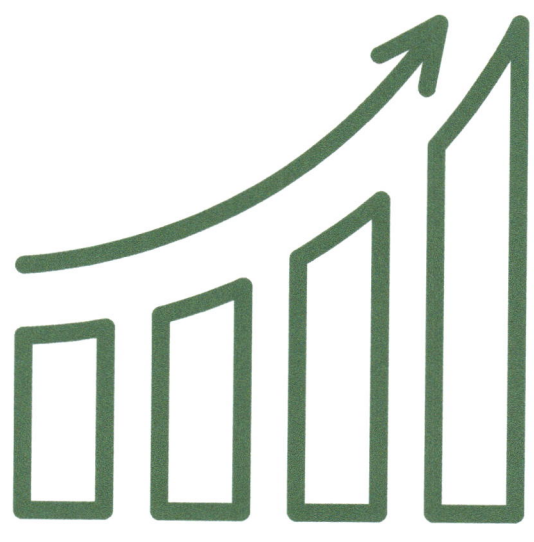

CONDITIONS THAT AFFECT DEVELOPMENT

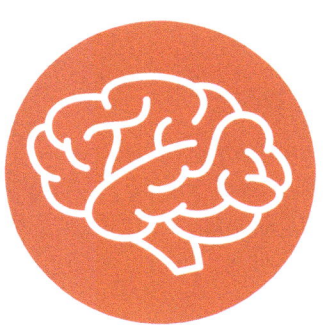

Autism Spectrum Disorder

This means a kid may have trouble talking with others, understanding feelings, and can do the same thing over and over again. They might really like a certain thing and focus on it a lot.

Down Syndrome

Down Syndrome: This happens when a child is born with an extra chromosome that slows down their growth and makes it harder for them to learn. They may look a little different, might have heart problems, and it might be tougher for them to remember things.

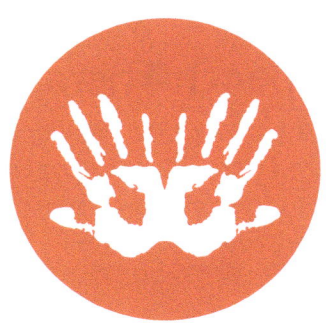

Attention Deficit Hyperactivity Disorder (ADHD)

Get enough sleep, exercise regularly, eat right, and learn how to manage stress in healthy ways. Learning how to manage stress in healthy ways ensures you have the energy to keep pushing forward.

Learning Disability

This is when a child might learn slower or have trouble doing daily activities and getting along with others. It could be because of genetics, problems at birth, getting very sick, or being around harmful things.

Cerebral Palsy

This can make it harder for a child to move their body. They might struggle with walking, holding things, keeping their balance, or sitting up straight.

30

COMMON TREATMENTS FOR DEVELOPMENTAL DELAYS

Early Intervention Programs

These are special programs for kids who are younger than five. They help the kid get better at thinking, talking, playing with others, moving, and learning to do things for themselves.

Speech Therapy

This helps kids who have trouble speaking or understanding language. Speech therapists can assists with pronunciation problems, improve the flow of speech, and help kids to understand and express themselves better.

Behavior Therapies

When kids have trouble with behaviors, talking, or socializing, behavior therapies like Applied Behavior Analysis (ABA) can help. Therapists teach kids how to behave, talk, and socialize. They also teach thinking skills. They work hard to reduce bad behaviors and increase good ones.

Occupational Therapy

This therapy helps kids with everyday tasks, like eating, getting dressed, and taking care of themselves. It also helps kids with playing and making friends.

Physical Therapy

This helps kids get better at moving and balancing. It can make their muscles stronger and make them better at doing things like walking, sitting, and standing. Sometimes, kids might need tools to help them, and the therapist will teach them how to use these.

31

UNDERSTANDING SAFETY RISKS IN TODDLERS WITH DEVELOPMENTAL DELAYS

Things that can show that toddlers may have slow growth include doing unsafe things like

- Harmful: They might hit, bite, or kick others. Or they may throw fits. They might act this way because they feel upset or can't say what they need.
- Trouble Talking: They might not know or be able to follow basic safety rules. This can lead to danger.
- Always on the Go: Toddlers with delays can be very active and make decisions quickly without thinking, leading to bumps or accidents.
- Running Away: Toddlers with developmental conditions may wander or run away which can put them at risk.
- Eating Things That Aren't Food: Sometimes toddlers might try to eat things like toys or dirt, which can cause choking or poisoning.
- Not Understanding Danger: A lot of toddlers with delays might not know what things are risky and could get injured.

MAKE DOCTOR VISIT IF

Here are only some of the reasons you want to take your child in right away for a doctors visit

- **Fever That Stays**: If your little one has a really high fever you should probably take them to the doctor.
- **Breathing Weird:** If your toddler has a hard time breathing, is breathing too fast, or their nostrils are flaring out, don't ignore this. It's best to call the doctor.
- **Cough That Won't Stop:** If your toddler has been coughing and it's getting worse, they need to see a doctor.
- **Throwing Up A Lot/Diarrhea:** If your kid is throwing up or has diarrhea a lot of times in one day, they should see a doctor. It might mean something more serious.
- **Won't Eat or Drink:** If your toddler isn't eating or drinking for a whole day, call a doctor. They might be getting dehydrated.
- **Showing Signs of Being Too Dry**: If your little one has a dry mouth, no tears when crying, eyes looking sunken, or feels really tired, it might mean they're dehydrated and need a doctor right away.
- **Rashes or Sores on Skin:** If there are weird rashes, bruises, or sores on your child's skin that don't go away after a few days, it could be an infection.
- **Pain That Won't Go Away:** If your child tells you something hurts, or you see them avoiding using a certain part of their body for more than a day, talk to a doctor.
- **Acting Different:** If your child is very sleepy, fussy, or just not acting like themselves, you might want to see the doctor.
- **Not Growing Like Other Kids**: If your toddler isn't doing things like walking, talking, or playing like other kids their age, you should talk to a pediatrician, a doctor who knows a lot about kids.

Remember, if you're ever unsure about whether or not you should take your toddler to the doctor, it's better to be safe than sorry.

PRACTICE LABELING COMMON ITEMS WITH YOUR CHILD

To help your child learn, use a book with pictures to show them different things and talk about them. It's okay if they don't talk back right away, just keep trying. Be calm and happy when you talk to them because it helps them learn better. Remember, learning takes time, so be happy with the small steps your child makes. Always say nice things to make them feel good and want to learn more. If you're worried about how they're doing, ask a teacher or expert for advice.

PRACTICE LABELING COMMON FOOD ITEMS

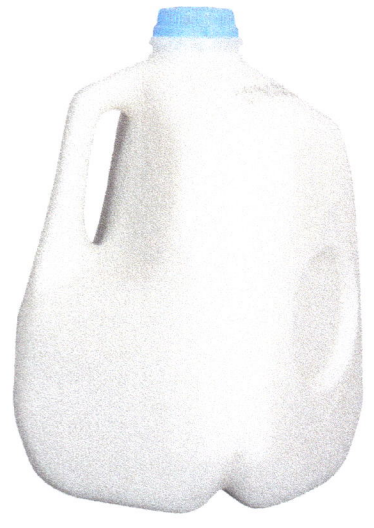

PRACTICE LABELING FOODS ITEMS

PRACTICE LABELING FOOD ITEMS

PRACTICE LABELING COMMON PLAY ITEMS

PRACTICE LABELING FOR OF TRANSPORTATION

PRACTICE LABELING CLOTHING ITEMS

PRACTICE LABELING COMMON CLOTHING

PRACTICE LABELING COMMON HOUSEHOLD ITEMS

PRACTICE LABELING COMMON HOUSEHOLD ITEMS

PRACTICE LABELING COMMON HOUSEHOLD ITEMS

PRACTICE LABELING HOUSE FEATURES

PRACTICE LABELING COMMON INSECTS

PRACTICE LABELING BATHROOM ITEMS

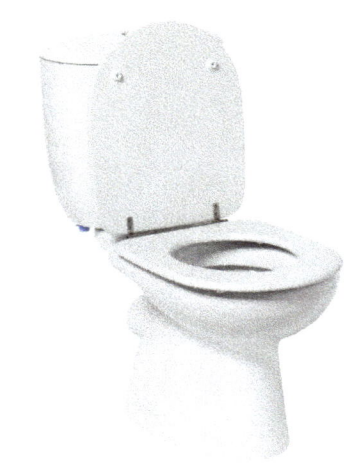

PRACTICE LABELING BODY PARTS

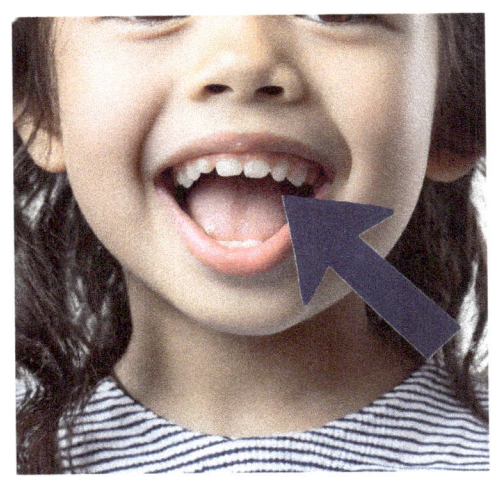

PRACTICE LABELING BODY PARTS

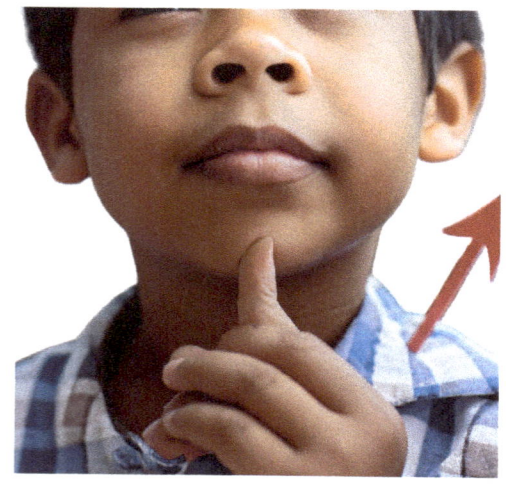 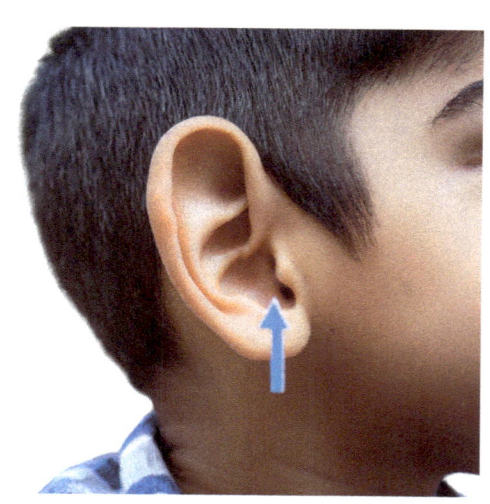

PRACTICE LABELING BODY PARTS

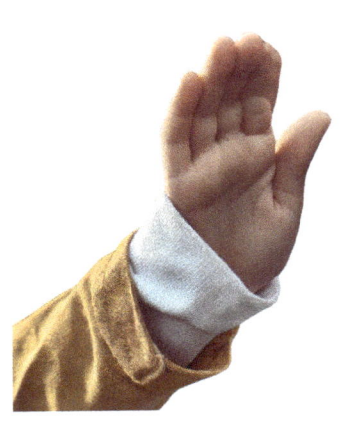
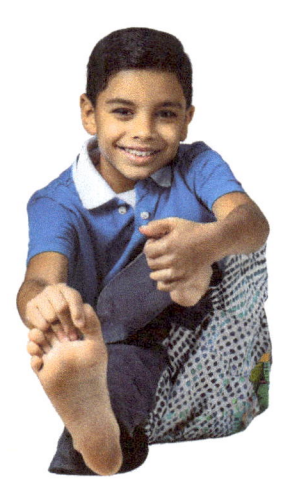

PRACTICE LABELING EMOTIONS

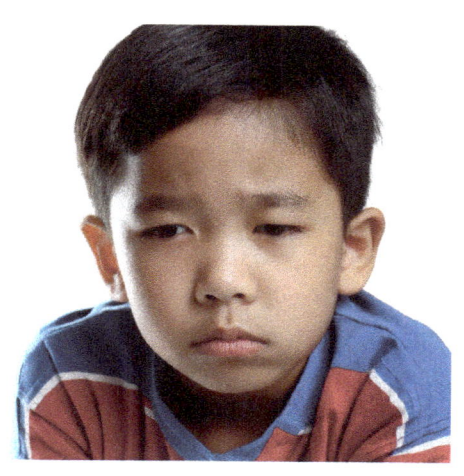

PRACTICE LABELING ANIMALS

PRACTICE LABELING ANIMALS

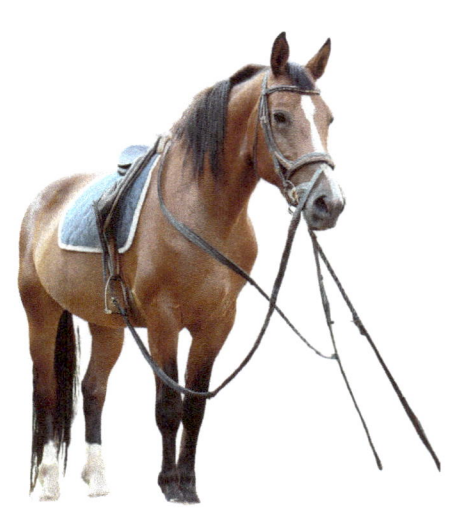

PRACTICE LABELING SPECIES

PRACTICE LABELING PLANTS

PRACTICE LABELING ANIMALS

PRACTICE LABELING COMMON ITEMS

PRACTICE LABELING COMMUNITY VECHILES

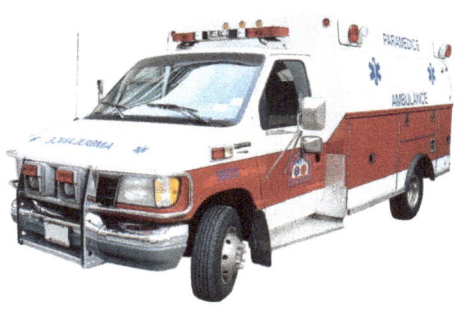

PRACTICE LABELING SHAPES & COLORS

PRACTICE LABELING SHAPES & COLORS

PRACTICE LABELING COMMUNITY HELPERS

PRACTICE LABELING COMMUNITY HELPERS

TEACH YOUR CHILD ABC'S AND 123'S

Teaching your child ABC's and 123's is important and fun. Start with singing the alphabet song together and counting objects around the house like toys and spoons. Use colorful books and games to make learning exciting. Remember, practice makes perfect, so keep it up every day.

PRACTICE LABELING ABC'S

Aa	Bb	Cc
Dd	Ee	Ff

PRACTICE LABELING ABC'S

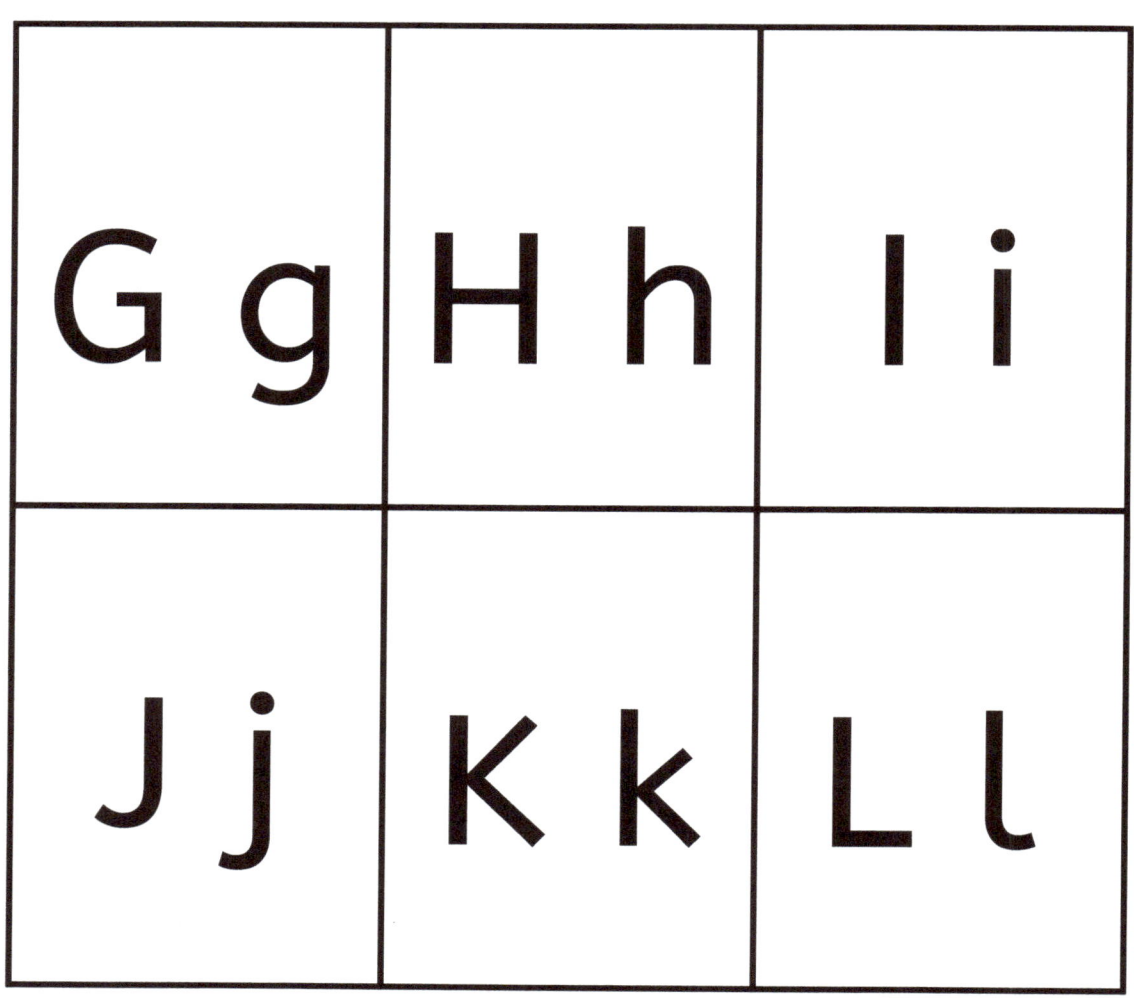

G g	H h	I i
J j	K k	L l

PRACTICE LABELING ABC'S

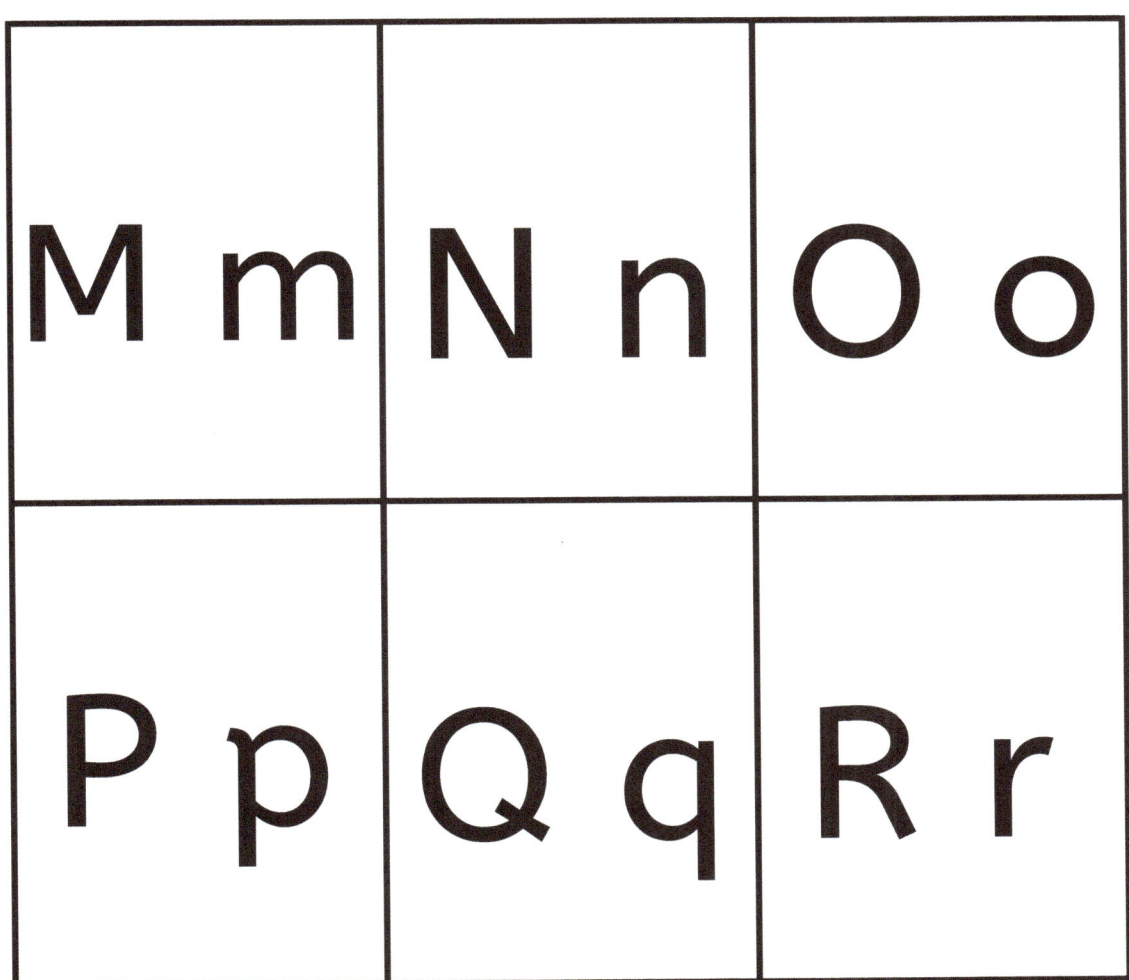

M m	N n	O o
P p	Q q	R r

PRACTICE LABELING ABC'S

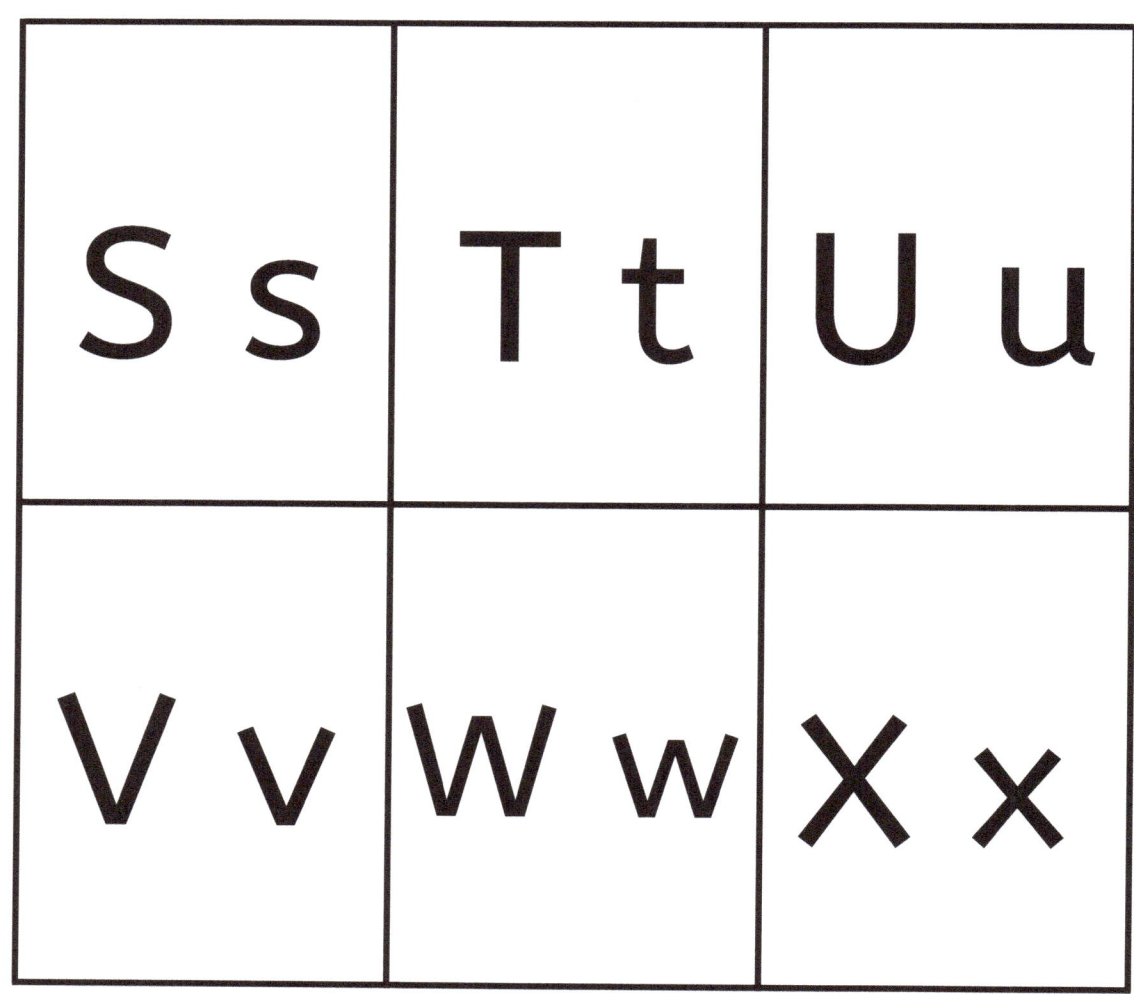

Ss	Tt	Uu
Vv	Ww	Xx

PRACTICE LABELING ABC'S

Y y	Z z	

PRACTICE LABELING 123'S

1	2	3
4	5	6

PRACTICE LABELING NUMBER'S

7	8	9
10	11	12

PRACTICE LABELING NUMBERS

13	14	15
16	17	18

PRACTICE LABELING NUMBER'S

19	20	21
22	23	24

THE CONTENTS OF THIS GUIDE ARE INSPIRED FROM THE FOLLOWING SOURCES

National Institute of Mental Health. (n.d.). Autism Spectrum Disorder. Retrieved from https://www.nimh.nih.gov/health/publications/autism-spectrum-disorder

National Institute of Mental Health. (n.d.). Attention-Deficit/Hyperactivity Disorder (ADHD). Retrieved from https://www.nimh.nih.gov/health/topics/attention-deficit-hyperactivity-disorder-adhd

National Institute of Mental Health. (2022). Toddlers' Responses to Baby Talk Linked to Social, Cognitive, Language Abilities. Retrieved from https://www.nimh.nih.gov/news/science-news/2022/toddlers-responses-to-baby-talk-linked-to-social-cognitive-language-abilities

National Institute of Mental Health. (n.d.). Children and Mental Health. Retrieved from https://www.nimh.nih.gov/health/publications/children-and-mental-health

Eunice Kennedy Shriver National Institute of Child Health and Human Development. (n.d.). Down Syndrome. Retrieved from https://www.nichd.nih.gov/health/topics/downsyndrome

Eunice Kennedy Shriver National Institute of Child Health and Human Development. (n.d.). Publications & Products. Retrieved from https://www.nichd.nih.gov/publications/product/20

Eunice Kennedy Shriver National Institute of Child Health and Human Development. (n.d.). Learning Disabilities. Retrieved from https://www.nichd.nih.gov/health/topics/learningdisabilities

National Center for Biotechnology Information. (2021). Genes and Disease [Book]. Retrieved from https://www.ncbi.nlm.nih.gov/books/NBK568743/

National Institute on Deafness and Other Communication Disorders. (n.d.). Speech and Language. Retrieved from https://www.nidcd.nih.gov/health/speech-and-language

National Center for Biotechnology Information. (2022). [Article on Speech and Language Development]. Retrieved from https://www.ncbi.nlm.nih.gov/pmc/articles/PMC10106707/

National Center for Biotechnology Information. (2015). [Article on Language Development Disorders]. Retrieved from https://www.ncbi.nlm.nih.gov/pmc/articles/PMC4461833/

National Center for Biotechnology Information. (2012). [Article on Speech Development]. Retrieved from https://www.ncbi.nlm.nih.gov/pmc/articles/PMC3289766/

National Center for Biotechnology Information. (2011). [Article on Communication Disorders]. Retrieved from https://www.ncbi.nlm.nih.gov/pmc/articles/PMC3088085/

National Center for Biotechnology Information. (2017). [Article on ADHD]. Retrieved from https://www.ncbi.nlm.nih.gov/pmc/articles/PMC5645046/

National Center for Biotechnology Information. (2019). [Book on Pediatric Care]. Retrieved from https://www.ncbi.nlm.nih.gov/books/NBK459146/

National Center for Biotechnology Information. (2020). [Book on Child Development]. Retrieved from https://www.ncbi.nlm.nih.gov/books/NBK562231/

National Center for Biotechnology Information. (2017). [Book on Disorders in Childhood]. Retrieved from https://www.ncbi.nlm.nih.gov/books/NBK279295/

National Institute of Dental and Craniofacial Research. (n.d.). A Healthy Mouth for Your Baby. Retrieved from https://catalog.nidcr.nih.gov/catalog/healthy-mouth-your-baby

Zero to Three (n.d.). Promoting Social Emotional Development: Tips on Nurturing Your Child's Curiosity.

ACKNOWLEDGEMENTS

This guide has been created for the amazing children of Michigan, aiming to help parents boost their child's overall development and to support parents. I thank my colleagues, partnering organizations, and mentors for their help during my studies and with this project. Also, a special thanks to my family and children for playing a crucial role and for their constant encouragement.

DISCLOUSE STATEMENT

Tammy McCrory MA LLP, BCBA, LBA authored McCrory's Developmental Milestones Express Tool Kit and recognizes potential conflicts of interest from promoting this book. Holding licenses as a Limited Licensed Psychologist and a Board Certified and Licensed Behavior Analyst, McCrory's book draws from her expertise, potentially benefiting her financially through related consulting and speaking engagements.

Endorsements for the book may enhance McCrory's professional reputation and indirectly benefit her practice. The book recommends specific tools and interventions and while these are based on evidence and professional opinion, there is a potential perceived benefit for McCrory.

McCrory retains intellectual property rights over the book's content, further representing a financial interest. However, efforts have been made to ensure an objective presentation of content, aligning with current research and evidence-based practices.

McCrory is committed to transparency and aims to avoid undue influence on the book's content by any financial or professional affiliations. The disclosure is made to inform readers and the professional community, underlining her intent to contribute to the field's advancement while acknowledging possible conflicts of interest.

You may contact the offer via email contact@tammymccrory.com